■SCHOLAST

Now I Know My

WORD FAMILIES
Learning Mats

50+ Double-Sided Activity Sheets That Help Children Read, Write, and Learn the Top Word Families

Lucia Kemp Henry

New York • Toronto • London • Auckland • Sydney
Mexico City • New Delhi • Hong Kong • Buenos Aires

Teaching
Resources

Edited by Immacula A. Rhodes
Cover design by Scott Davis
Interior illustrations by Lucia Kemp Henry
Interior design by Holly Grundon

ISBN: 978-0-545-39703-2

2 3 4 5 6 7 8 9 10   40   19 18 17 16 15 14

Contents

Learning Mats

Short Vowels

Long Vowels With Silent e

Other Long Vowel Phonograms

Mat	Skill
65–66	Word Family: -*ail*
67–68	Word Family: -*ain*
69–70	Word Family: -*ay*
71–72	Word Family: -*eat*
73–74	Word Family: -*ee*
75–76	Word Family: -*eel*
77–78	Word Family: -*eet*
79–80	Word Family: -*ight*
81–82	Word Family: -*oat*
83–84	Word Family: -*ow*

Variant Vowels

Mat	Skill
85–86	Word Family: -*all*
87–88	Word Family: -*aw*
89–90	Word Family: -*ook*
91–92	Word Family: -*ool*
93–94	Word Family: -*oot*

Diphthongs and R-Controlled Vowels

Mat	Skill
95–96	Word Family: -*oil*
97–98	Word Family: -*own*
99–100	Word Family: -*ar*
101–102	Word Family: -*ore*
103–104	Word Family: -*orn*

About This Book

Welcome to *Now I Know My Word Families Learning Mats*! The double-sided mats in this book provide engaging activities designed to help children master more than 50 different word families. In addition, the systematic format reinforces emerging reading and fine-motor skills while enabling children to work independently.

The interactive, reproducible mats feature appealing art and simple, predictable text that targets key phonograms that have short and long vowels, variant vowels, diphthongs, and *r*-controlled vowels. Activities include practice in recognizing and writing sound-spelling patterns, identifying words that belong to specific word families, matching words to pictures, and drawing related word-family pictures. The drawing and writing exercises help develop and strengthen fine-motor skills as well as reinforce the shape and formation of letters. And, as children read and follow directions to complete each mat, they build important word recognition and comprehension skills. To help meet the learning needs of your students, check page 8 to see how activities in this book connect to the Common Core State Standards for Reading (Foundational Skills) and Language.

Preparing and using the learning mats is quick and easy! Simply make double-sided copies to use for instruction with the whole class, small groups, student pairs, or individuals. The mats are also ideal for independent work, centers, and homework. You'll find that daily practice with these activities helps build word-decoding skills, fluency, comprehension, and other early literacy skills. Best of all, children will experience the joy of learning as they develop skills that help them grow into more confident, fluent readers.

What's Inside

Each ready-to-go learning mat in this resource targets a specific word family. To use, simply decide on the phonogram you want to teach, locate the corresponding mats in the book, and make a double-sided copy of the selected mats. The only materials kids need for the activities are crayons or colored pencils. To use, children read and follow the directions to perform each activity. You'll find the following activities on the mats:

❖ **Write the Word:** To practice writing, spelling, recognizing, and sounding-out words that belong to the same word family, children fill in the letters to complete each word. When finished, encourage them to note the sound and spelling pattern of the words.

❖ **Identify the Word:** Children identify and color items that belong to the target word family.

✤ **Word and Picture Match:** Boost word recognition as children draw lines to match each word to its picture.

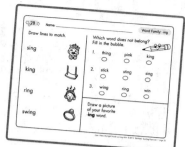

✤ **Bubble It In:** To practice letter-sound and discrimination skills, children read a series of words, then fill in the bubble for the word that does not belong. This activity also gives them practice with the format of many standardized tests.

✤ **Draw Your Favorite:** Children illustrate their favorite word that belongs to the target word family. They might draw a picture of something already represented on the mat, or choose another related word.

Helpful Tips

The following suggestions will help you and your students get the most out of the learning mats:

• Complete each mat in advance to become familiar with the directions, art, and response for each activity. If desired, laminate your completed copy to use as an answer key. (Or slip the mat into a clear, plastic page protector.) You might bind all of your answer keys into a notebook to keep on hand for children to check their work.

• Use the mats to introduce new concepts, track children's progress in mastering essential skills, and review concepts already covered.

• Prepare the mats for repeated use in learning centers. Simply laminate the double-sided mats and put them in a center along with wipe-off color crayons and paper towels (to use as erasers).

• Compile sets of the learning mats into booklets for children to complete in class or at home. For example, you might staple copies of mats 1–10 between two sheets of construction paper and title the booklet, "My Book of Short *a* Word Families."

• The mats are also perfect for instant homework assignments. Send the pages home with children to complete. This is an easy way to reinforce skills covered in class as well as to help keep families informed about what their children are learning, what they've mastered, and where they might need some extra guidance.

Word Family Learning Mats Reference List

Use this handy list as a reference for identifying pictures on the odd-numbered mats and for checking children's responses to the bubble-in activities on the even-numbered mats.

Mats 1–2: bag, cap, flag, tag, wag; 1. sad, 2. tap, 3. flap

Mats 3–4: fan, ham, jam, ram, yam; 1. ran, 2. yawn, 3. hum

Mats 5–6: can, cat, fan, pan, van; 1. run, 2. ham, 3. men

Mats 7–8: cap, map, pan, snap, trap; 1. mad, 2. sad, 3. cab

Mats 9–10: bat, can, cat, hat, mat; 1. man, 2. ten, 3. sit

Mats 11–12: bed, sad, shed, sled, wed; 1. bad, 2. weed, 3. lad

Mats 13–14: bell, doll, shell, spell, well; 1. pull, 2. spill, 3. fall

Mats 15–16: bed, hen, men, pen, ten; 1. hand, 2. tan, 3. pin

Mats 17–18: bus, chest, nest, vest, west; 1. mast, 2. bust, 3. rent

Mats 19–20: hat, jet, net, vet, wet; 1. sat, 2. got, 3. pat

Mats 21–22: brick, chick, kick, pig, stick; 1. pig, 2. chin, 3. tock

Mats 23–24: dig, dog, pig, twig, wig; 1. kick, 2. get, 3. wick

Mats 25–26: bin, chin, fin, kite, pin; 1. fine, 2. find, 3. pine

Mats 27–28: king, pin, ring, swing, wing; 1. pink, 2. stick, 3. win

Mats 29–30: hit, knit, pin, pit, sit; 1. fin, 2. kid, 3. bite

Mats 31–32: block, clock, lock, pot, sock; 1. soak, 2. look, 3. float

Mats 33–34: dog, frog, jog, log, sock; 1. lock, 2. bag, 3. pig

Mats 35–36: hop, mop, stamp, stop, top; 1. pod, 2. hot, 3. map

Mats 37–38: boat, cot, hot, knot, pot; 1. hat, 2. pet, 3. goat

Mats 39–40: cup, buck, duck, stuck, truck; 1. pack, 2. tick, 3. back

Mats 41–42: bug, dog, mug, plug, rug; 1. dog, 2. red, 3. jog

Mats 43–44: drum, dump, jump, pump, stump; 1. drum, 2. down, 3. job

Mats 45–46: bunk, junk, skunk, sock, trunk; 1. dark, 2. honk, 3. spark

Mats 47–48: bag, cake, lake, rake, snake; 1. talk, 2. snack, 3. back

Mats 49–50: bale, ball, sale, scale, whale; 1. pole, 2. whole, 3. tall

Mats 51–52: flame, frame, game, ham, same; 1. come, 2. time, 3. fan

Mats 53–54: bike, dice, ice, mice, price; 1. slide, 2. mine, 3. right

Mats 55–56: bride, chick, hide, ride, slide; 1. nine, 2. dive, 3. time

Mats 57–58: line, nine, pin, spine, vine; 1. dime, 2. pin, 3. tie

Mats 59–60: hole, mole, pole, soap, tadpole; 1. wall, 2. stale, 3. mile

Mats 61–62: bone, comb, cone, phone, throne; 1. lawn, 2. bun, 3. come

Mats 63–64: close, dress, hose, nose, rose; 1. note, 2. pass, 3. claws

Mats 65–66: ball, pail, sail, snail, tail; 1. maid, 2. rain, 3. pain

Mats 67–68: brain, chain, pan, rain, train; 1. star, 2. maid, 3. raid

Mats 69–70: hay, jay, spray, train, tray; 1. pain, 2. claw, 3. trail

Mats 71–72: heat, jet, meat, seat, wheat; 1. team, 2. heal, 3. seam

Mats 73–74: bee, jay, tee, three, tree; 1. week, 2. feed, 3. need

Mats 75–76: eel, heel, peel, tree, wheel; 1. fell, 2. read, 3. bell

Mats 77–78: beet, feet, jeep, meet, street; 1. sheep, 2. bean, 3. tree

Mats 79–80: knight, light, night, right, tie; 1. rent, 2. sting, 3. mint

Mats 81–82: boat, coat, float, gate, goat; 1. flat, 2. soap, 3. got

Mats 83–84: bone, bow, crow, row, snow; 1. gown, 2. now, 3. throne

Mats 85–86: ball, bell, fall, tall, wall; 1. smell, 2. mail, 3. tale

Mats 87–88: claw, crown, paw, saw, straw; 1. jam, 2. lawn, 3. star

Mats 89–90: book, cook, hook, lock, look; 1. knock, 2. talk, 3. crack

Mats 91–92: doll, pool, school, spool, stool; 1. foul, 2. tall, 3. doll

Mats 93–94: boot, hoot, pot, root, toot; 1. shot, 2. hot, 3. toad

Mats 95–96: boil, coil, mole, oil, soil; 1. call, 2. tail, 3. all

Mats 97–98: clown, crown, frown, phone, town; 1. yawn, 2. our, 3. claw

Mats 99–100: bar, bear, car, jar, star; 1. tan, 2. care, 3. tear

Mats 101–102: core, score, snore, sore, star; 1. bar, 2. pole, 3. phone

Mats 103–104: acorn, corn, four, horn, thorn; 1. barn, 2. won, 3. more

Meeting the Standards

Connections to the Common Core State Standards

The Common Core State Standards Initiative (CCSSI) has outlined learning expectations in English/Language Arts for students at different grade levels. The activities in this book align with the following standards for students in grades K–2. For more information, visit the CCSSI Web site at www.corestandards.org.

Reading Standards: Foundational Skills

Print Concepts

- RF.K.1, RF.1.1. Demonstrate understanding of the organization and basic features of print.

- RF.K.1a. Recognize and name all upper- and lowercase letters of the alphabet.

Phonological Awareness

- RF.K.2, RF.1.2. Demonstrate understanding of spoken words, syllables, and sounds (phonemes).

- RF.K.2a. Recognize and produce rhyming words.

- RF.K.2b. Count, pronounce, blend, and segment syllables in spoken words.

- RF.K.2c. Blend and segment onsets and rimes of single-syllable spoken words.

- RF.K.2d. Isolate and pronounce the initial, medial vowel, and final sounds (phonemes) in three-phoneme (consonant-vowel-consonant, or CVC) words.

- RF.K.2e. Add or substitute individual sounds (phonemes) in simple, one-syllable words to make new words.

- RF.1.2 a. Distinguish long from short vowel sounds in spoken single-syllable words.

- RF.1.2 b. Orally produce single-syllable words by blending sounds (phonemes), including consonant blends.

- RF.1.2 c. Isolate and pronounce initial, medial vowel, and final sounds (phonemes) in spoken single-syllable words.

- RF.1.2 d. Segment spoken single-syllable words into their complete sequence of individual sounds (phonemes).

Phonics and Word Recognition

- RF.K.3, RF.1.3, RF.2.3. Know and apply grade-level phonics and word analysis skills in decoding words.

- RF.K.3a. Demonstrate basic knowledge of letter-sound correspondences by producing the primary or most frequent sound for each consonant.

- RF.K.3b. Associate the long and short sounds with the common spellings (graphemes) for the five major vowels.

- RF.K.3c. Read common high-frequency words by sight (e.g., *the, of, to, you, she, my, is, are, do, does*).

- RF.K.3d. Distinguish between similarly spelled words by identifying the sounds of the letters that differ.

- RF.1.3a. Know the spelling-sound correspondences for common consonant digraphs (two letters that represent one sound).

- RF.1.3b. Decode regularly spelled one-syllable words.

- RF.1.3c. Know final -e and common vowel team conventions for representing long vowel sounds.

- RF.1.3g. Recognize and read grade-appropriate irregularly spelled words.

- RF.2.3a. Distinguish long and short vowels when reading regularly spelled one-syllable words.

- RF.2.3c. Decode regularly spelled two-syllable words with long vowels.

- RF.2.3f. Recognize and read grade-appropriate irregularly spelled words.

Fluency

- RF.K.4, RF.1.4, RF.2.4. Read with sufficient accuracy and fluency to support comprehension.

- RF.1.4a, RF.2.4a. Read grade-level text with purpose and understanding.

- RF.1.4c, RF.2.4c. Use context to confirm or self-correct word recognition and understanding, rereading as necessary.

Language

Conventions of Standard English

- L K.1, L.1.1, L.2.1. Demonstrate command of the conventions of standard English grammar and usage when writing or speaking.

- L K. 1a, L.1.1a. Print upper- and lowercase letters.

- L.K.2, L.1.2, L.2.2. Demonstrate command of the conventions of standard English capitalization, punctuation, and spelling when writing.

Name: _____

Write words that end with **-ag.**

Color each item that ends with **-ag.**

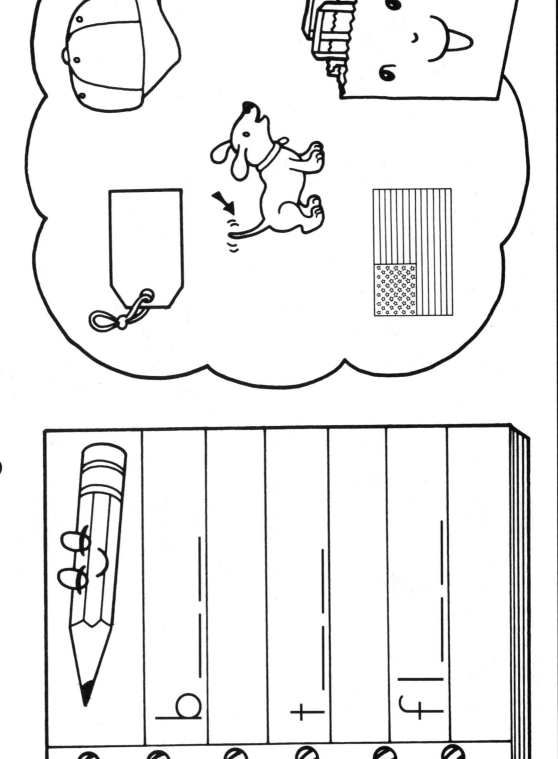

b __ __

t __ __

fl __ __

Which word does not belong? Fill in the bubble.

1. sad ○   rag ○   bag ○

2. drag ○   tag ○   tap ○

3. wag ○   flap ○   flag ○

Draw a picture of your favorite **-ag** word.

Name:

2

Draw lines to match.

wag

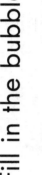

flag

tag

bag

Name: _____

3

Write words that end with **-am.**

Color each item that ends with **-am.**

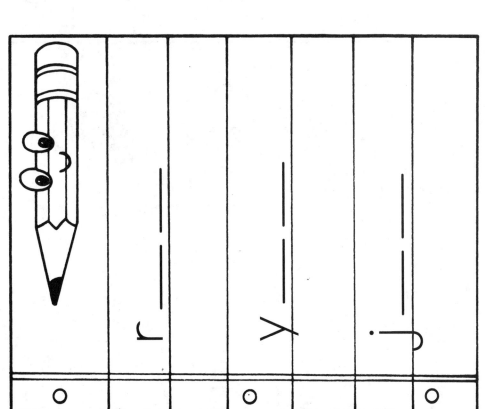

Which word does not belong? Fill in the bubble.

1. slam ○   ran ○   ram ○

2. yawn ○   yam ○   clam ○

3. ham ○   jam ○   hum ○

Draw a picture of your favorite **-am** word.

Name: _____

Draw lines to match.

ram

yam

jam

ham

★ ★ ★ 5

Name: _____

Write words that end with -**an**.

Color each item that ends with -**an**.

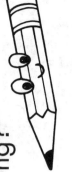

Which word does not belong?
Fill in the bubble.

1.	run ○	van ○	ran ○
2.	man ○	tan ○	ham ○
3.	can ○	men ○	fan ○

Draw a picture
of your favorite
-an word.

☆ 6
☆☆

Name: _____

Draw lines to match.

fan

pan

van

can

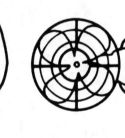

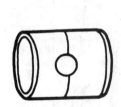

Name: _____

7

Write words that end with **-ap.**

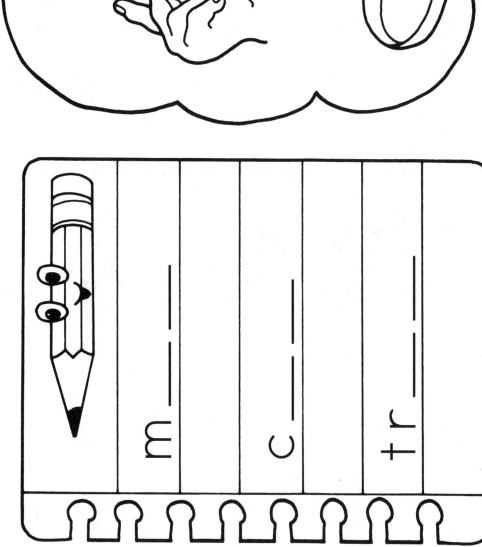

m _____

c _____

t r _____

Color each item that ends with **-ap.**

Name: _____

☆ 8 ☆

Draw lines to match.

map

cap

snap

trap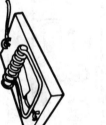

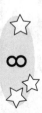

Which word does not belong?
Fill in the bubble.

1. ○ map   ○ mad   ○ clap

2. ○ sad   ○ lap   ○ trap

3. ○ nap   ○ slap   ○ cab

Draw a picture
of your favorite
-ap word.

Name: _____

☆ 9 ☆
☆

Write words that end with -**at**.

Color each item that ends with -**at**.

Welcome

c _ _

m _ _

b _ _

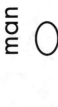

Name: _____

☆ 10 ☆☆

Draw lines to match.

mat

cat

bat

hat

Which word does not belong?
Fill in the bubble.

1. ◯ mat   ◯ hat   ◯ man

2. ◯ that   ◯ fat   ◯ ten

3. ◯ sit   ◯ bat   ◯ sat

Draw a picture of your favorite -at word.

☆ ☆ 11
☆ ☆

Name: _____

Write words that end with -**ed**.

Color each item that ends with -**ed**.

b e d

w e d

s l e d

Which word does not belong? Fill in the bubble.

1. bed ⬤   red ⬤   bad ◯
2. fed ⬤   weed ⬤   wed ⬤
3. lad ◯   led ⬤   shed ⬤

Draw a picture of your favorite **-ed** word.

12 ☆

Name: _____

Draw lines to match.

bed

sled

wed

shed

Color each item that ends with -**ell**.

☆ 13 ☆☆

Name: _____

Write words that end with -**ell**.

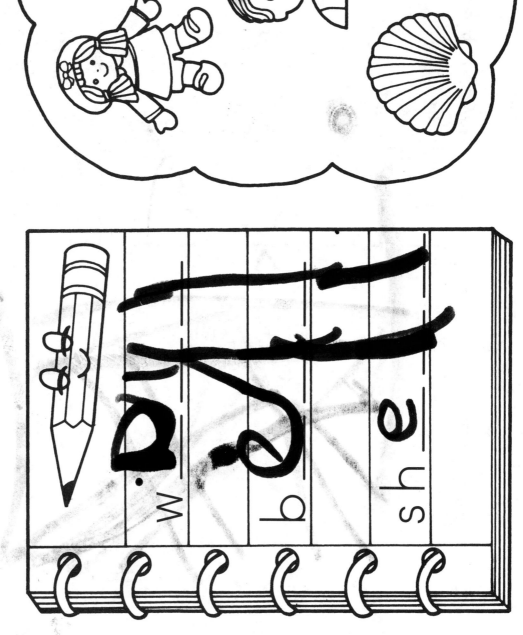

Name: _____

14

Which word does not belong?
Fill in the bubble.

well ⬤

shell ◯

fall ◯

1.

tell ◯

spill ⬤

sell ◯

2. spell ◯

3. fell ◯

pull ⬤

Draw a picture
of your favorite
-ell word.

Draw lines to match.

well

shell

bell

spell

Name: _____

15 ⭐⭐⭐

Write words that end with -**en**.

Color each item that ends with -**en**.

h e n

t e n

p e n

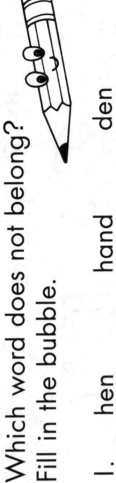

Which word does not belong?
Fill in the bubble.

1.	hen ○	hand ○	den ○
2.	tan ○	when ○	ten ○
3.	men ○	pen ○	pin ○

Draw a picture
of your favorite
-en word.

Name: _____

☆ 16 ☆

Draw lines to match.

men

hen

ten

pen

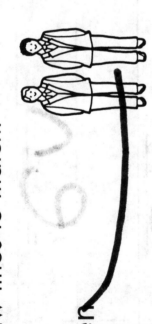

Name: _____

17

Write words that end with -**est**.

Color each item that ends with -**est**.

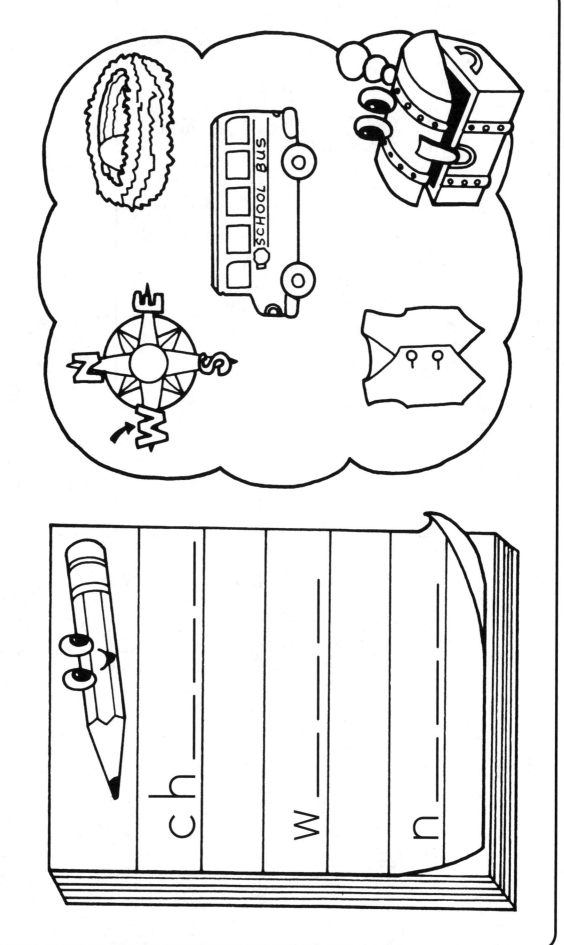

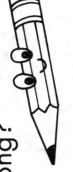

Which word does not belong?
Fill in the bubble.

1. ○ pest ○ mast ○ test

2. ○ bust ○ nest ○ best

3. ○ rest ○ chest ○ rent

Draw a picture
of your favorite
-est word.

★ 18 ★

Name: _____

Draw lines to match.

west

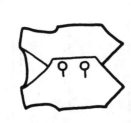

vest

nest

chest

☆ 19 ☆
☆

Name: _____

Color each item that ends with -**et**.

Write words that end with -**et**.

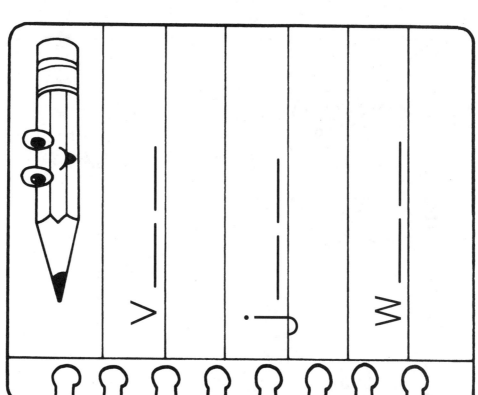

v _ _

j _ _

w _ _

Name: _____

☆ 20 ☆

Draw lines to match.

wet

vet

jet

net

Which word does not belong?
Fill in the bubble.

1. sat ○   let ○   net ○

2. get ○   yet ○   got ○

3. wet ○   pat ○   pet ○

Draw a picture of your favorite -et word.

Name: _____

☆ 21 ☆

Write words that end with -**ick.**

Color each item that ends with -**ick.**

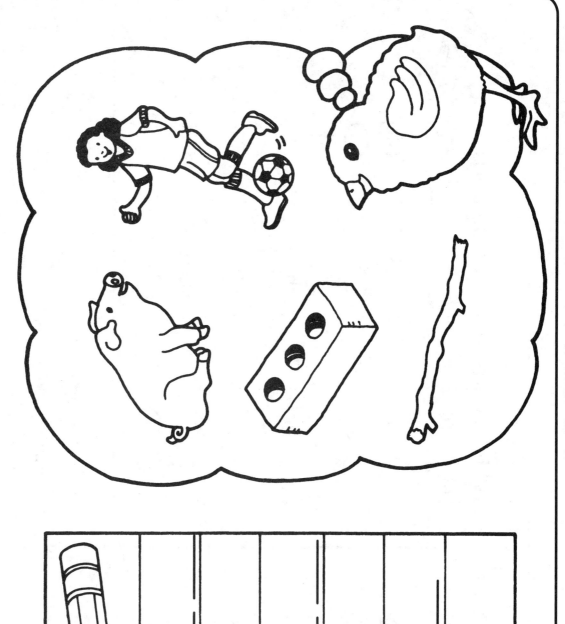

ch ____

br ____

k ____

☆ 22 ☆

Name: _____

Draw lines to match.

brick

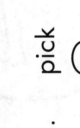

kick

chick

stick

Which word does not belong?
Fill in the bubble.

1. pick ◯   trick ◯   pig ◯

2. sick ◯   chin ◯   chick ◯

3. tock ◯   stick ◯   tick ◯

Draw a picture
of your favorite
-ick word.

☆ **23** ☆☆

Name: _____

Color each item that ends with **-ig**.

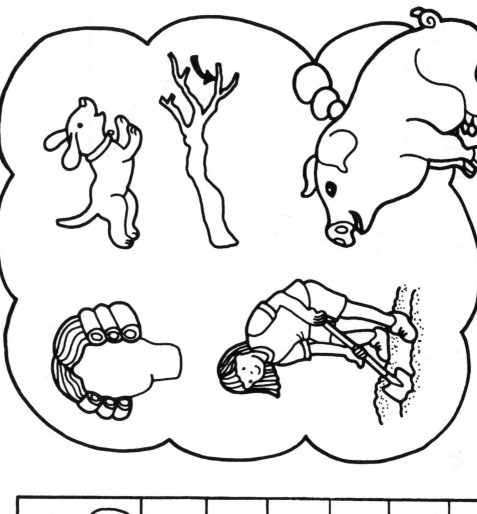

Write words that end with **-ig**.

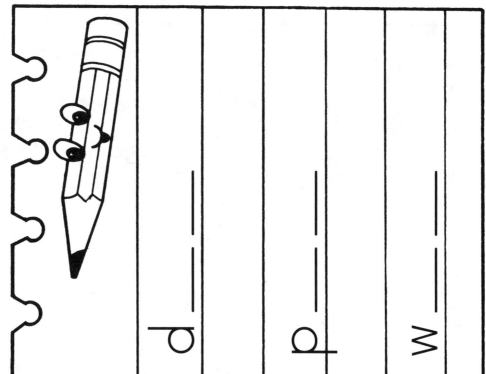

d _ _

p _ _

w _ _

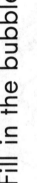

Name: _____

Which word does not belong?
Fill in the bubble.

1. pig ◯   kick ◯   big ◯

2. get ◯   fig ◯   twig ◯

3. wig ◯   dig ◯   wick ◯

Draw a picture
of your favorite
-ig word.

★24 ☆
☆★

Draw lines to match.

twig

dig

pig

wig

Name: _____

Color each item that ends with **-in**.

Write words that end with **-in**.

f _ _

p _ _

b _ _

Name: _____

Draw lines to match.

chin

pin

bin

fin

Which word does not belong?
Fill in the bubble.

1. fine ◯   win ◯   grin ◯

2. spin ◯   fin ◯   find ◯

3. tin ◯   pine ◯   pin ◯

Draw a picture
of your favorite
-in word.

☆27☆

Name: _____

Write words that end with -ing.

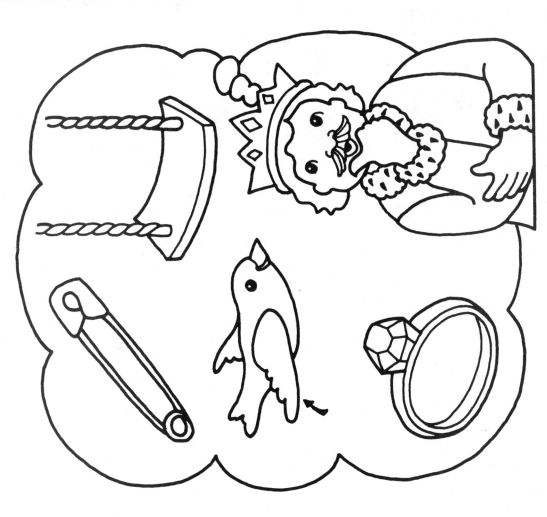

r _ _ _

k _ _ _

w _ _ _

Color each item that ends with -ing.

Name: _____

⭐ 28 ⭐

Draw lines to match.

sing

king

ring

swing

Which word does not belong?
Fill in the bubble.

1. ○ thing   ○ pink   ○ king

2. ○ stick   ○ sting   ○ sing

3. ○ wing   ○ ring   ○ win

Draw a picture
of your favorite
-ing word.

Name: _____

☆ 29 ☆
☆

Write words that end with -**it**.

Color each item that ends with -**it**.

☆30☆ Name: _____

Draw lines to match.

knit

hit

pit

sit

Which word does not belong?
Fill in the bubble.

1. fit ◯   sit ◯   fin ◯

2. kit ◯   kid ◯   hit ◯

3. bite ◯   bit ◯   knit ◯

Draw a picture
of your favorite
-it word.

☆ 31
☆ ☆

Name: _____

Write words that end with -**ock**.

Color each item that ends with -**ock**.

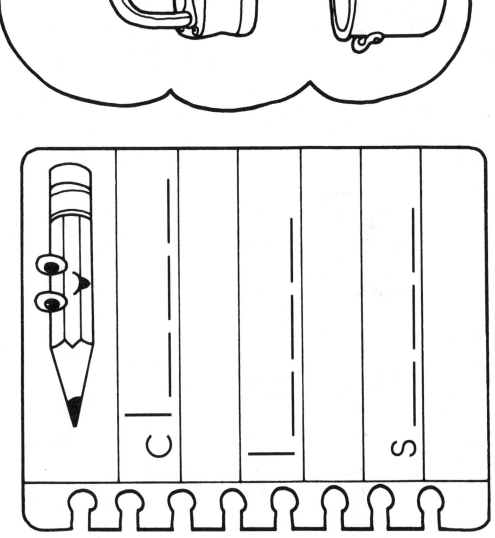

c_l _____

_l _____

s_____

Name: _____

32 ☆

Draw lines to match.

clock

lock

block

sock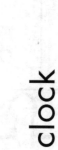

Which word does not belong?
Fill in the bubble.

1. soak ○   knock ○   sock ○

2. rock ○   lock ○   look ○

3. dock ○   float ○   flock ○

Draw a picture
of your favorite
-ock word.

33

Name: _____

Write words that end with **-og**.

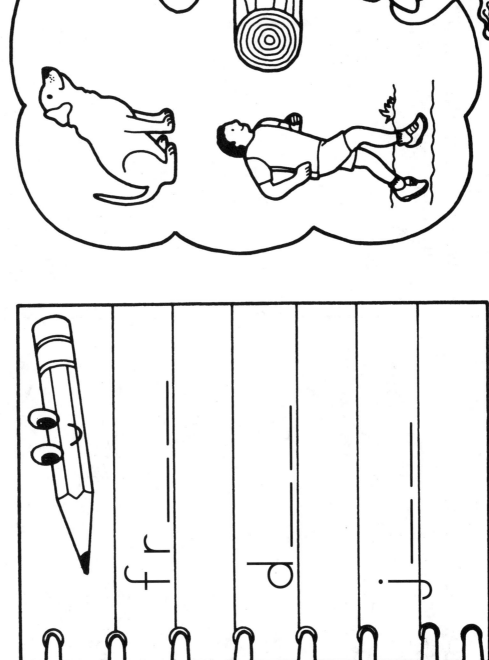

Color each item that ends with **-og**.

Name: _____

☆ 34 ☆

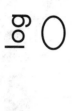

Which word does not belong?
Fill in the bubble.

1. hog ○   lock ○   log ○

2. bag ○   bog ○   smog ○

3. dog ○   jog ○   pig ○

Draw a picture
of your favorite
-og word.

Draw lines to match.

log

frog

dog

jog

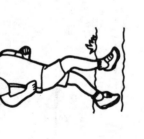

Name: _____

Write words that end with -**op**.

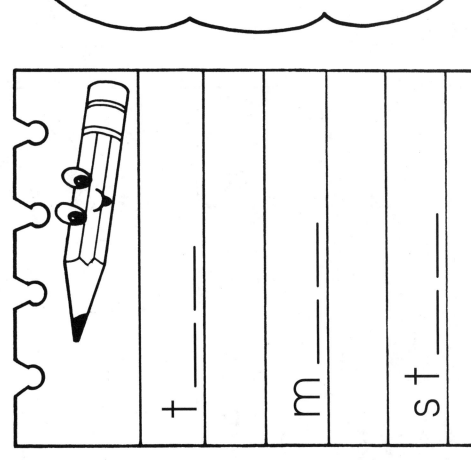

t __ __

m __ __

s t __ __

Color each item that ends with -**op**.

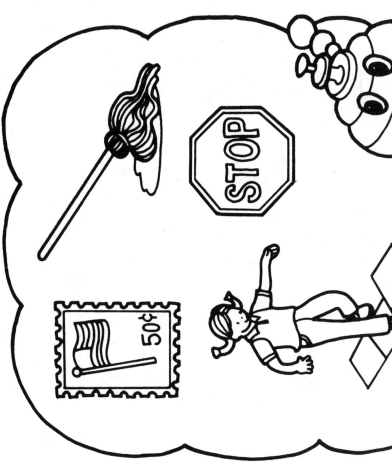

STOP

50¢

Which word does not belong?
Fill in the bubble.

1. pop ○   drop ○   pod ○

2. chop ○   hot ○   hop ○

3. map ○   top ○   mop ○

Draw a picture
of your favorite
-op word.

Name: _____

Draw lines to match.

top

hop

stop

mop

Color each item that ends with -**ot**.

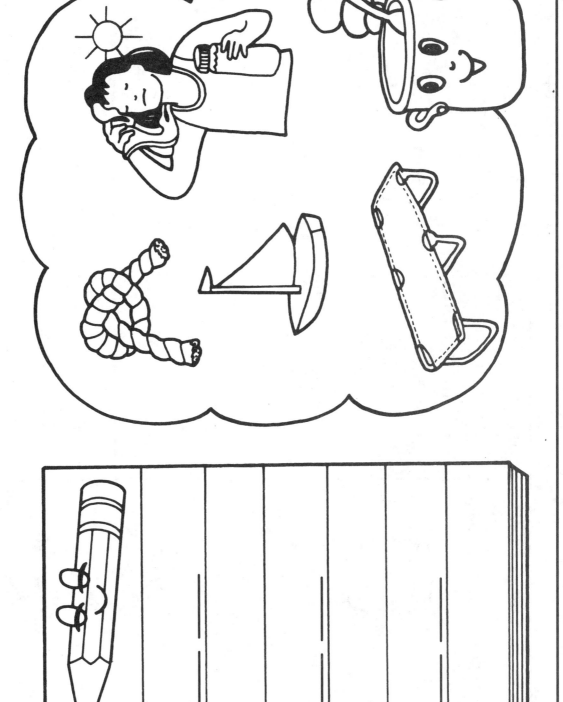

Name: _____

37

Write words that end with -**ot**.

p _ _

h _ _

c _ _

Name: _____

Which word does not belong?
Fill in the bubble.

1. dot ◯   hat ◯   hot ◯

2. pet ◯   slot ◯   pot ◯

3. knot ◯   got ◯   goat ◯

Draw a picture
of your favorite
-ot word.

⭐ **38** ⭐

Draw lines to match.

pot

hot

cot

knot

☆ 39 ☆
☆

Name: _____

Write words that end with **-uck**.

Color each item that ends with **-uck**.

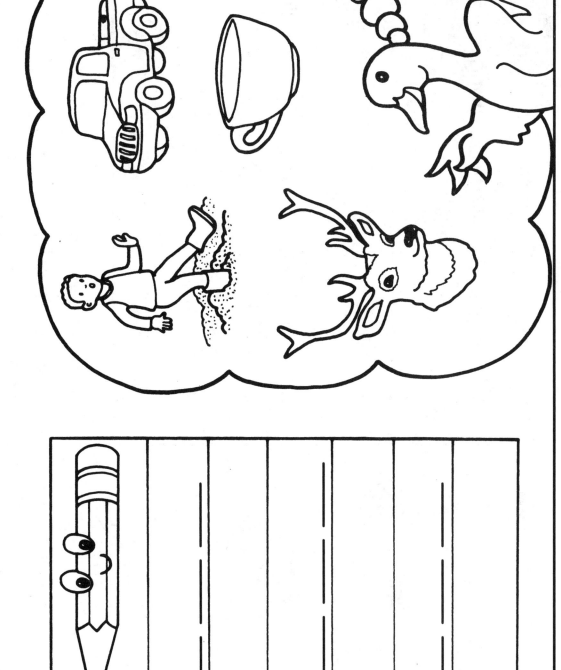

☆ 40 ☆
☆

Name: _____

Draw lines to match.

duck

stuck

truck

buck

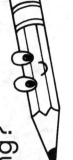

Which word does not belong?
Fill in the bubble.

1.	pack ○	luck ○	puck ○
2.	tick ○	tuck ○	duck ○
3.	muck ○	back ○	buck ○

Draw a picture
of your favorite
-uck word.

Name: _____

Write words that end with -**ug**.

Color each item that ends with -**ug**.

r _ _

p _ _ _

m _ _ _

41

☆42☆

Name: _____

Draw lines to match.

rug

mug

plug

bug

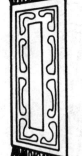

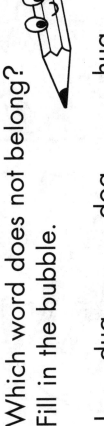

Which word does not belong?
Fill in the bubble.

1. dug ○   dog ○   hug ○

2. red ○   rug ○   tug ○

3. bug ○   jug ○   jog ○

Draw a picture
of your favorite
-ug word.

Name: _____

43

Write words that end with -**ump**.

Color each item that ends with -**ump**.

p _____

s t _____

j _____

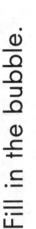

Which word does not belong?
Fill in the bubble.

1. drum ⭕   bump ⭕   lump ⭕

2. hump ⭕   dump ⭕   down ⭕

3. jump ⭕   job ⭕   pump ⭕

Draw a picture
of your favorite
-ump word.

---

44 ☆

Name: _____

Draw lines to match.

dump

stump

pump

jump

☆ 45 ☆
☆

Name: _____

Write words that end with **-unk.**

Color each item that ends with **-unk.**

s k __ __

b __ __ __

j __ __ __

46

Name: _____

Draw lines to match.

skunk

junk

trunk

bunk

Which word does not belong?
Fill in the bubble.

1. dunk ◯ dark ◯ skunk ◯

2. honk ◯ hunk ◯ chunk ◯

3. spunk ◯ junk ◯ spark ◯

Draw a picture
of your favorite
-unk word.

Name: _____

Write words that end with **-ake**.

Color each item that ends with **-ake**.

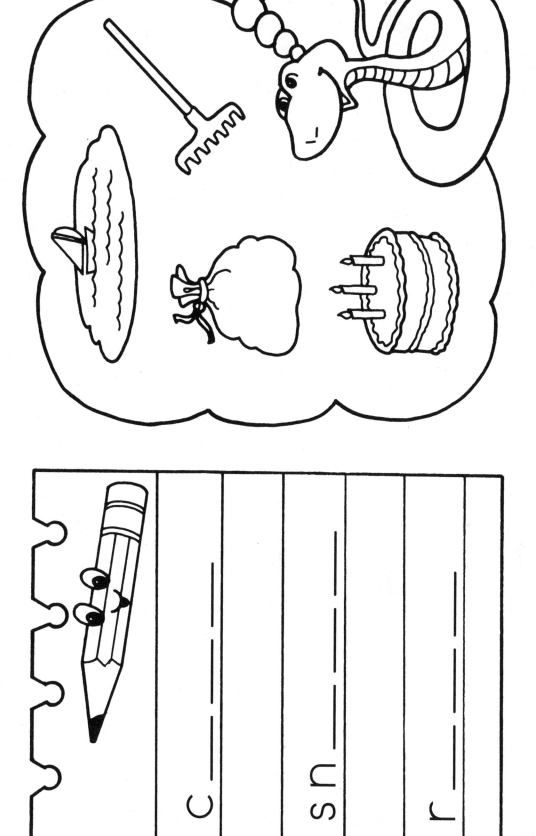

c _ _ _

s _ _ _

n _ _ _

r _ _ _

☆ 48 ☆

Name: _____

Draw lines to match.

lake

rake

snake

cake

Which word does not belong?
Fill in the bubble.

1. ⚪ make   ⚪ talk   ⚪ take

2. ⚪ snack   ⚪ snake   ⚪ fake

3. ⚪ bake   ⚪ lake   ⚪ back

Draw a picture
of your favorite
-ake word.

Name: _____

49 ☆

Write words that end with **-ale.**

Color each item that ends with **-ale.**

$10.00
Now $5.00

w h _____

s _____

b _____

Which word does not belong?
Fill in the bubble.

1. pale ○   pole ○   bale ○

2. whale ○   stale ○   whole ○

3. male ○   tall ○   tale ○

Draw a picture
of your favorite
-ale word.

⭐ 50 ⭐

Name: _____

Draw lines to match.

whale

sale

scale

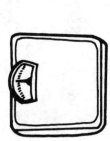

bale

51

Name: _____

Write words that end with **-ame.**

Color each item that ends with **-ame.**

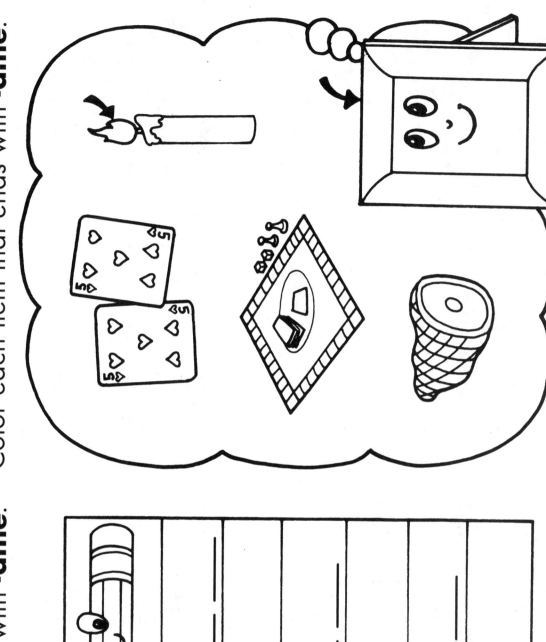

f r __ __ __

g __ __ __

s __ __ __

☆52☆

Name: _____

Draw lines to match.

game

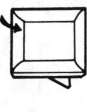

frame

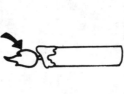

same

flame

Which word does not belong?
Fill in the bubble.

1. ○ came   ○ same   ○ come

2. ○ tame   ○ time   ○ lame

3. ○ fan   ○ blame   ○ fame

Draw a picture
of your favorite
-ame word.

Name: _____

☆53☆

Write words that end with -**ice.**

Color each item that ends with -**ice.**

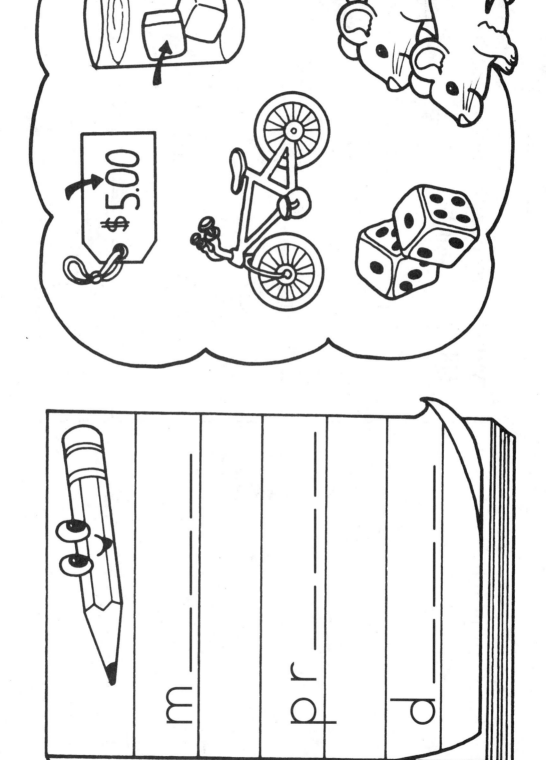

m _ _ _ _

p r _ _ _ _

d _ _ _ _

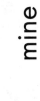

Which word does not belong?
Fill in the bubble.

1. slice ⬭   slide ⬭   dice ⬭

2. mice ⬭   spice ⬭   mine ⬭

3. twice ⬭   right ⬭   rice ⬭

Draw a picture
of your favorite
-ice word.

Name: _____

Draw lines to match.

price

ice

mice

dice

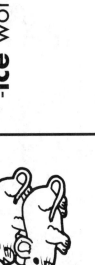

Name: _____

Write words that end with **-ide**.

Color each item that ends with **-ide**.

br _ _ _

h _ _ _

sl _ _ _

☆ 56 ☆

Name: _____

Draw lines to match.

ride

bride

hide

slide

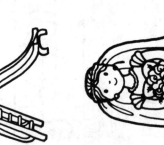

Which word does not belong?
Fill in the bubble.

1. ride ○   nine ○   hide ○

2. dive ○   side ○   wide ○

3. tide ○   glide ○   time ○

Draw a picture
of your favorite
-ide word.

Name: _____

57

Write words that end with **-ine.**

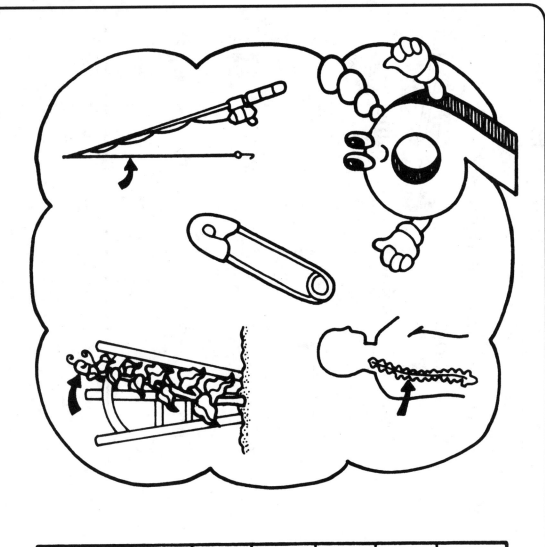

Color each item that ends with **-ine.**

n _____

v _____

sp _____

Name: _____

58

Draw lines to match.

vine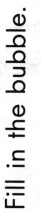

nine

line

spine

Which word does not belong?
Fill in the bubble.

1.	○ dime	○ dine	○ spine
2.	○ pine	○ mine	○ pin
3.	○ fine	○ tie	○ twine

Draw a picture
of your favorite
-ine word.

Name: _____

Write words that end with -**ole**.

Color each item that ends with -**ole**.

m _____

h _____

p _____

Which word does not belong?
Fill in the bubble.

1. whole ⚪   role ⚪   wall ⚪

2. stole ⚪   stale ⚪   pole ⚪

3. mile ⚪   mole ⚪   hole ⚪

Draw a picture
of your favorite
-ole word.

Name: _____

☆ 60 ☆

Draw lines to match.

pole

mole

hole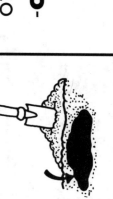

tadpole

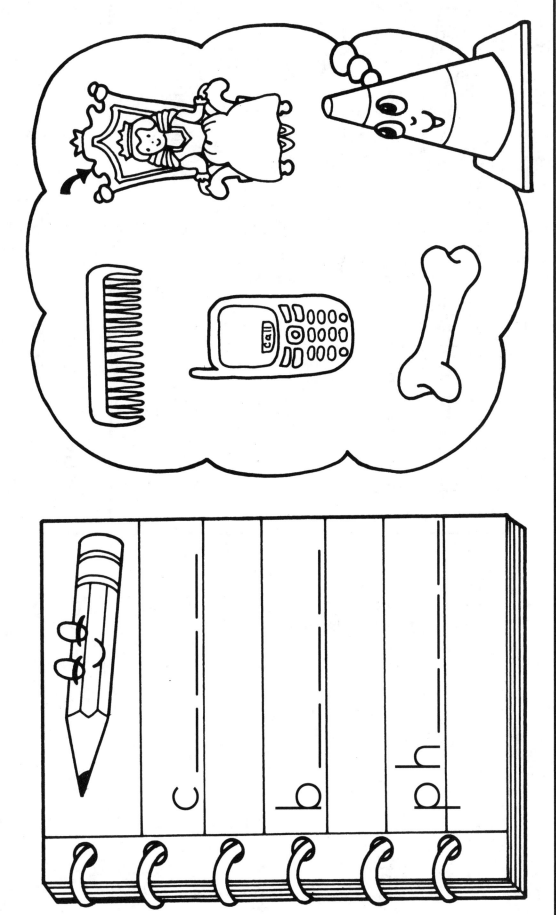

★ 61

Name: _____

Write words that end with **-one**.

Color each item that ends with **-one**.

Name: _____

Which word does not belong?
Fill in the bubble.

1. lawn ○   lone ○   tone ○

2. bone ○   phone ○   bun ○

3. cone ○   come ○   throne ○

Draw a picture
of your favorite
-one word.

☆ 62 ☆

Draw lines to match.

bone

throne

cone

phone

Name: _____

☆63☆

Write words that end with **-ose**.

Color each item that ends with **-ose**.

☆ 64 ☆

Name: _____

Draw lines to match.

nose

rose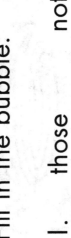

close

hose

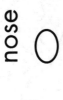

Which word does not belong?
Fill in the bubble.

1. ○ those   ○ note   ○ nose

2. ○ pass   ○ pose   ○ rose

3. ○ hose   ○ close   ○ claws

Draw a picture
of your favorite
-ose word.

☆65☆
☆

Name: _____

Write words that end with **-ail.**

Color each item that ends with **-ail.**

t _ _ _

p _ _ _

s _ _ _

Name: _____

Draw lines to match.

sail

pail

nail

snail

Which word does not belong?
Fill in the bubble.

1. nail ◯   maid ◯   mail ◯

2. trail ◯   rail ◯   rain ◯

3. pain ◯   bail ◯   sail ◯

Draw a picture
of your favorite
-ail word.

Name: _____

☆ 67 ☆

Write words that end with -**ain**.

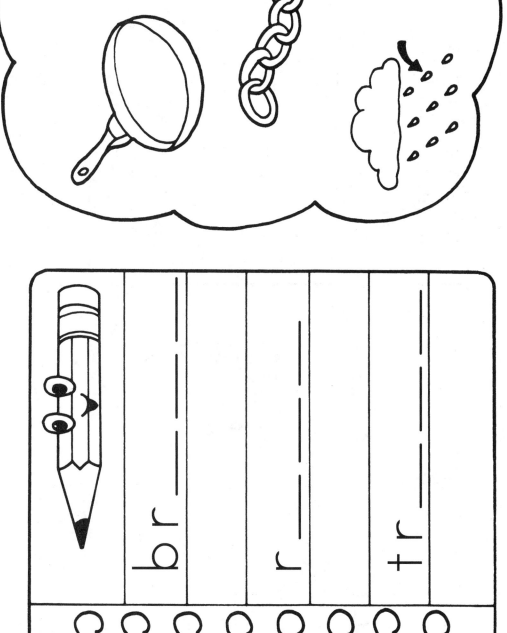

b r _ _ _

r _ _ _

t r _ _ _

Color each item that ends with -**ain**.

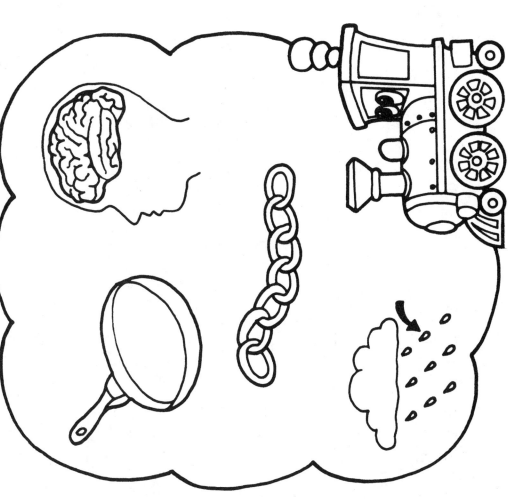

☆ 68 ☆

Name: _____

Draw lines to match.

chain

rain

train

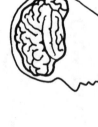

brain

Which word does not belong?
Fill in the bubble.

1.	stain ○	pain ○	star ○
2.	main ○	maid ○	train ○
3.	raid ○	rain ○	drain ○

Draw a picture
of your favorite
-ain word.

Name: _____

Write words that end with -**ay**.

Color each item that ends with -**ay**.

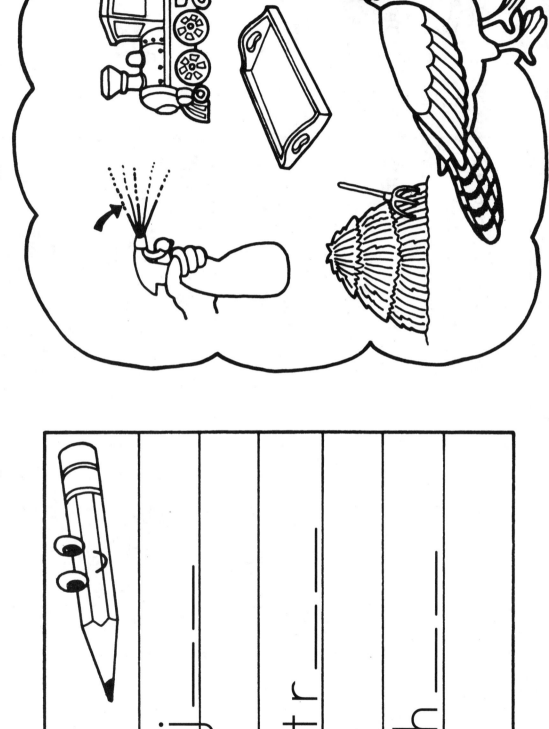

j _ _

tr _ _

h _ _

Name: _____

Draw lines to match.

tray

hay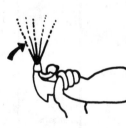

spray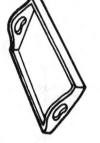

jay

Which word does not belong?
Fill in the bubble.

1. ◯ pain   ◯ day   ◯ pay

2. ◯ clay   ◯ may   ◯ claw

3. ◯ bay   ◯ trail   ◯ tray

Draw a picture
of your favorite
-ay word.

☆☆ 71 ☆☆

Name: _____

Write words that end with -**eat.**

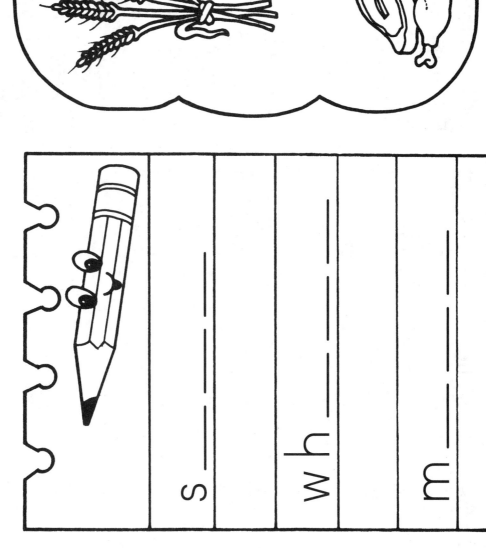

s _ _ _

w h _ _ _

m _ _ _

Color each item that ends with -**eat.**

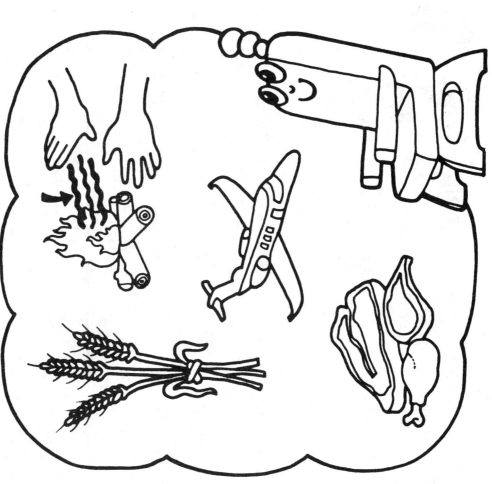

Name: _____

72

Draw lines to match.

heat

wheat

seat

meat

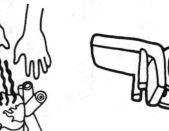

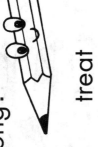

Which word does not belong?
Fill in the bubble.

1. ◯ meat   ◯ team   ◯ treat

2. ◯ heal   ◯ heat   ◯ beat

3. ◯ seat   ◯ wheat   ◯ seam

Draw a picture
of your favorite
-eat word.

Name: _____

Write words that end with -**ee**.

Color each item that ends with -**ee**.

t r __ __

b __ __ __

t __ __

3

Name: _____

74

Draw lines to match.

tee

bee

tree

three

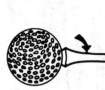

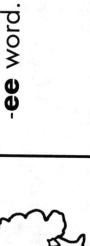

Which word does not belong?
Fill in the bubble.

1. knee ○   see ○   week ○

2. free ○   feed ○   tee ○

3. need ○   bee ○   three ○

Draw a picture
of your favorite
-ee word.

Name: _____

75

Write words that end with -**eel**.

Color each item that ends with -**eel**.

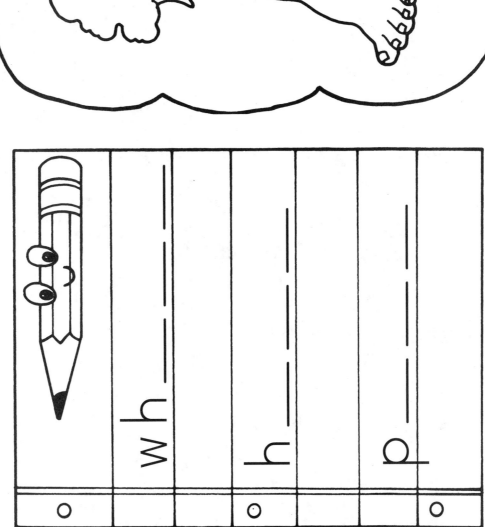

w h _ _ _

h _ _ _

p _ _ _

Name: _____

☆ 76 ☆

Draw lines to match.

peel

heel

eel

wheel

Which word does not belong?
Fill in the bubble.

1. ○ fell   ○ feel   ○ heel

2. ○ kneel   ○ reel   ○ read

3. ○ eel   ○ bell   ○ wheel

Draw a picture
of your favorite
-eel word.

☆ Name: _____

☆77☆

Write words that end with -**eet**.

Color each item that ends with -**eet**.

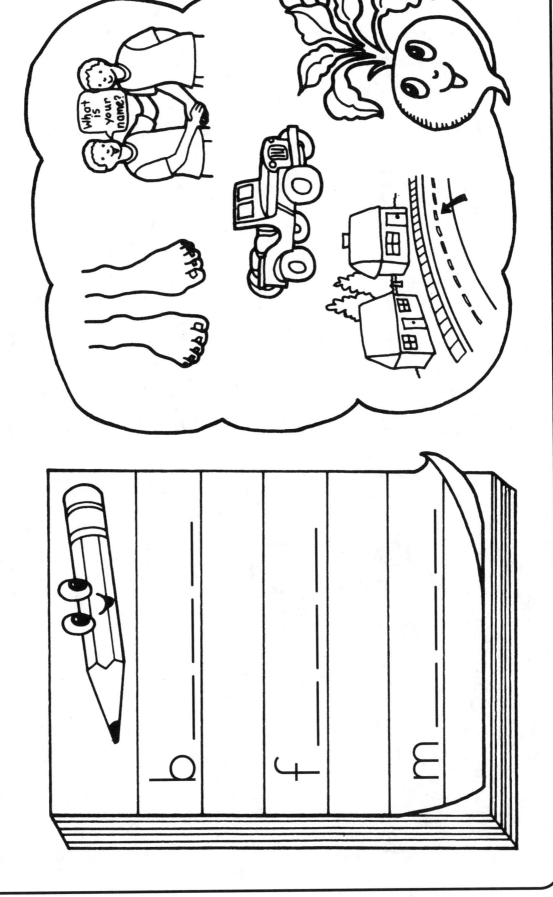

☆ 78 ☆

Name: _____

Draw lines to match.

feet

street

beet

meet

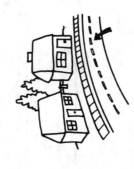
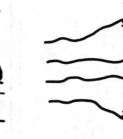

Which word does not belong?
Fill in the bubble.

1. sheet ◯   sheep ◯   greet ◯

2. bean ◯   tweet ◯   beet ◯

3. sweet ◯   street ◯   tree ◯

Draw a picture
of your favorite
-eet word.

⭐ 79

Name: _____

Write words that end with -**ight**.

Color each item that ends with -**ight**.

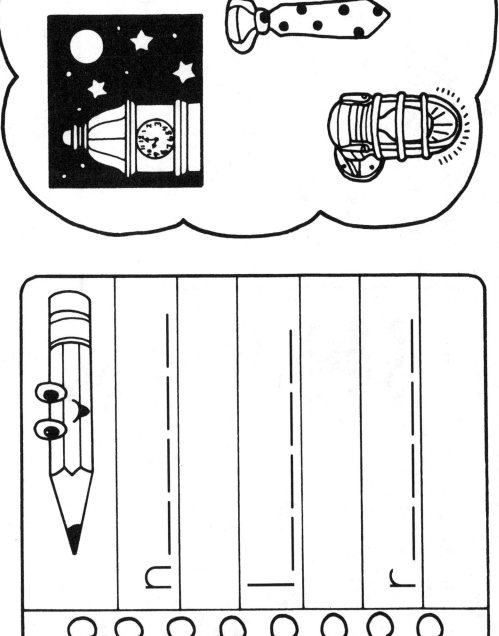

n _ _ _ _

l _ _ _ _

r _ _ _ _

Name: _____

Draw lines to match.

night

right

light

knight

Which word does not belong?
Fill in the bubble.

1. ○ fight   ○ right   ○ rent

2. ○ bright   ○ sting   ○ tight

3. ○ mint   ○ might   ○ night

Draw a picture
of your favorite
-ight word.

Name: _____

Color each item that ends with **-oat**.

Write words that end with **-oat**.

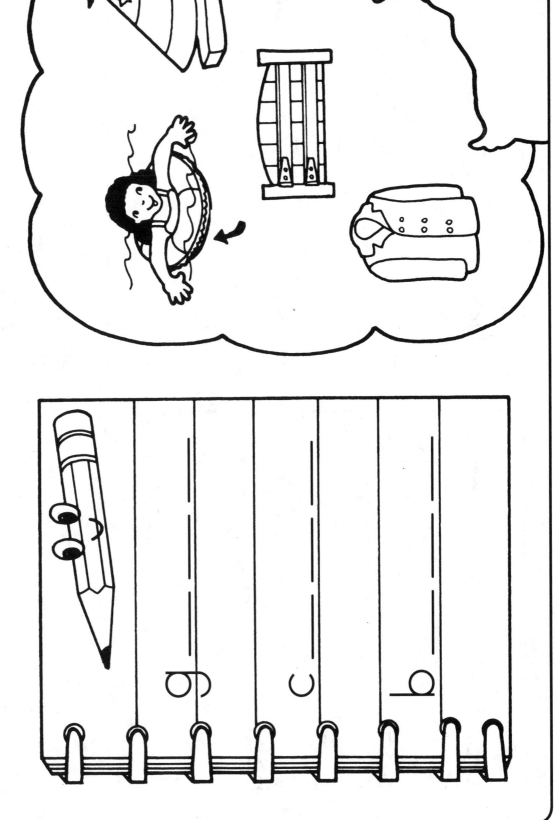

g____

c____

b____

Which word does not belong?
Fill in the bubble.

1. float ◯ flat ◯ boat ◯

2. soap ◯ moat ◯ oat ◯

3. throat ◯ goat ◯ got ◯

Draw a picture
of your favorite
-oat word.

☆ 82 ☆ Name: _____

Draw lines to match.

goat

coat

boat

float

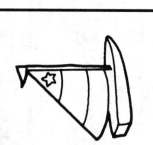

☆83☆

Name: _____

Write words that end with **-ow.**

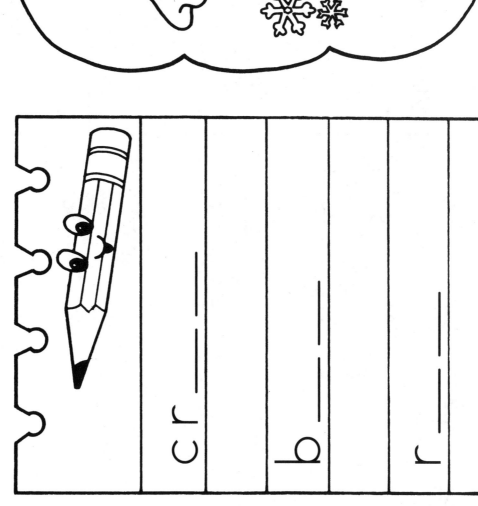

c r _ _

b _ _

r _ _

Color each item that ends with **-ow.**

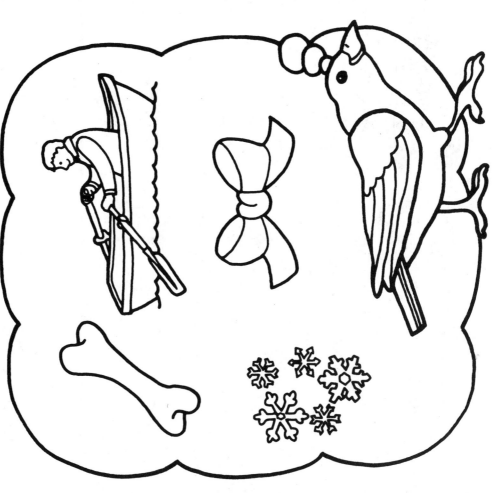

Name: _____

84

Draw lines to match.

snow

row

crow

bow

Which word does not belong?
Fill in the bubble.

1. low ○   gown ○   grow ○

2. now ○   snow ○   mow ○

3. throw ○   blow ○   throne ○

Draw a picture
of your favorite
-ow word.

Color each item that ends with **-all**.

☆ 85 ☆

Name: _____

Write words that end with **-all**.

b _ _ _ _ _

f _ _ _ _ _

w _ _ _ _ _

Name: _____

⭐86⭐

Draw lines to match.

tall

ball

wall

fall

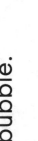
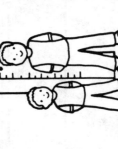

Which word does not belong?
Fill in the bubble.

1. small ⚪	smell ⚪	call ⚪
2. ball ⚪	mall ⚪	mail ⚪
3. hall ⚪	tale ⚪	tall ⚪

Draw a picture
of your favorite
-all word.

Name: _____

Write words that end with -**aw**.

Color each item that ends with -**aw**.

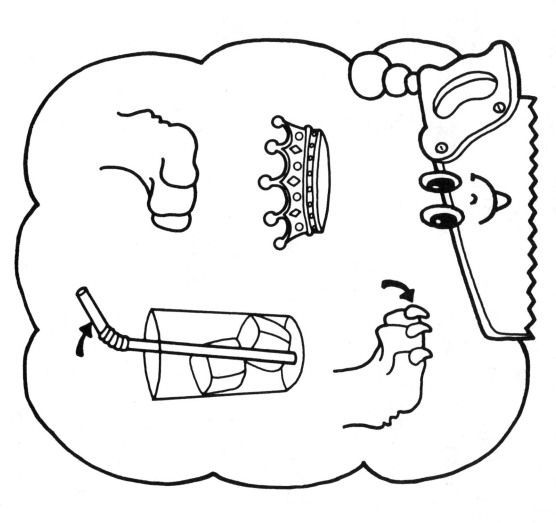

s _ _ _

p _ _ _

cl _ _ _

Name: _____

☆ 88 ☆

Draw lines to match.

paw

straw

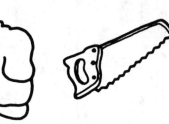

saw

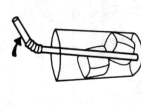

claw

Which word does not belong?
Fill in the bubble.

1. jaw ◯   claw ◯   jam ◯

2. law ◯   lawn ◯   saw ◯

3. star ◯   raw ◯   straw ◯

Draw a picture
of your favorite
-aw word.

Name: _____

Write words that end with **-ook**.

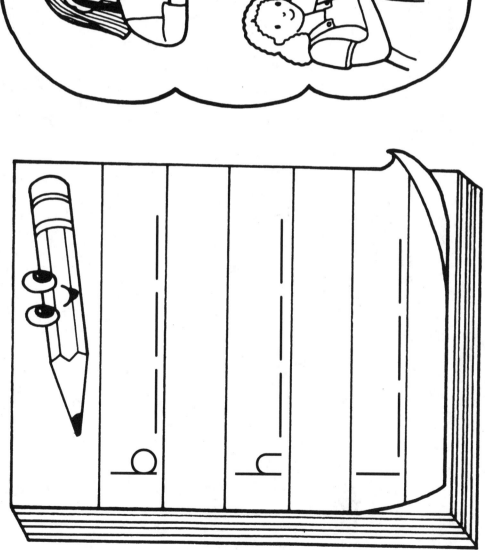

Color each item that ends with **-ook**.

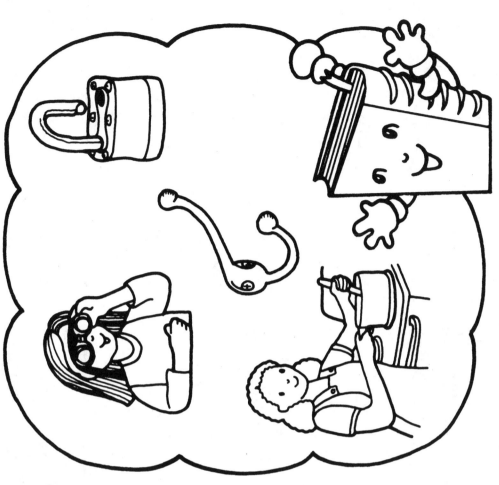

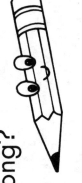

Which word does not belong?
Fill in the bubble.

1. knock ⟨○⟩   nook ⟨○⟩   brook ⟨○⟩

2. took ⟨○⟩   shook ⟨○⟩   talk ⟨○⟩

3. crook ⟨○⟩   crack ⟨○⟩   hook ⟨○⟩

Draw a picture
of your favorite
-ook word.

90

Name: _____

Draw lines to match.

cook

hook

book

look

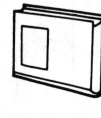

Name: _____

☆ 91 ☆
☆

Write words that end with -**ool**.

Color each item that ends with -**ool**.

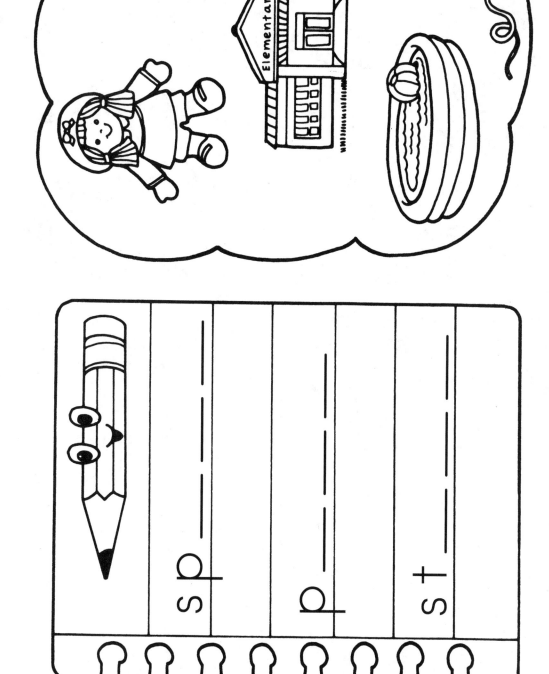

s p ___ ___ ___

p ___ ___ ___

s t ___ ___ ___

Name: _____

92

Draw lines to match.

school

pool

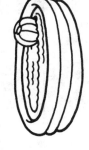

stool

spool

Which word does not belong?
Fill in the bubble.

1. ○ fool   ○ foul   ○ stool

2. ○ tool   ○ pool   ○ tall

3. ○ cool   ○ doll   ○ drool

Draw a picture of your favorite **-ool** word.

☆ Name: _____

93

Color each item that ends with **-oot**.

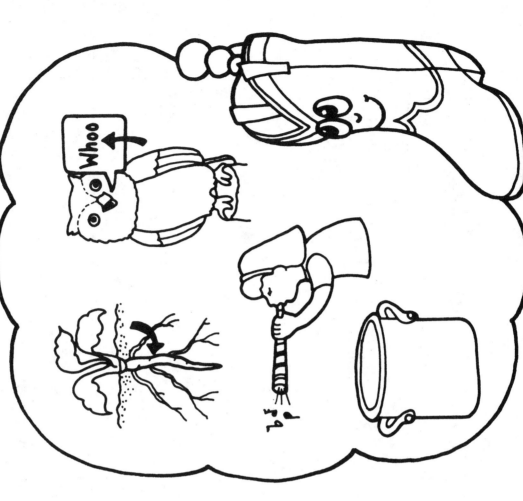

Write words that end with **-oot**.

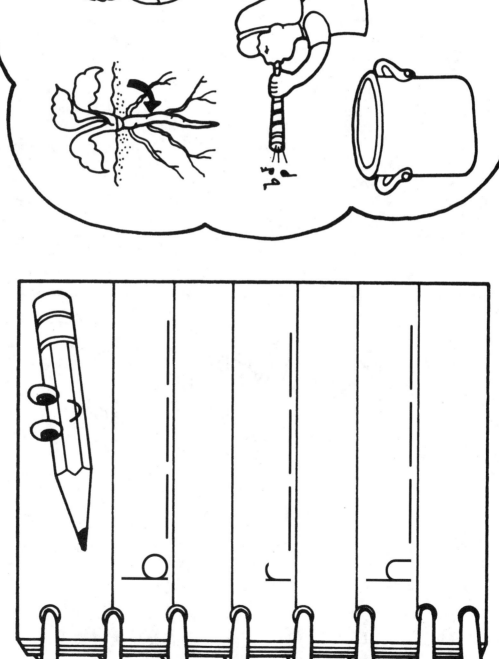

b___

r___

h___

☆94☆

Name: _____

Draw lines to match.

toot

boot

root

hoot

Which word does not belong?
Fill in the bubble.

1. ○ shoot ○ root ○ shot

2. ○ hoot ○ hot ○ loot

3. ○ toad ○ scoot ○ toot

Draw a picture of your favorite **-oot** word.

Name: _____

★ 95 ☆
☆ ☆

Write words that end with -**oil**.

Color each item that ends with -**oil**.

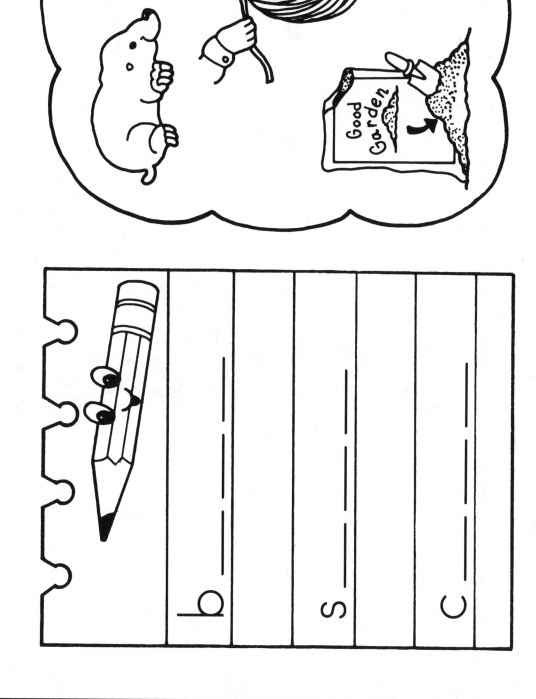

Good Garden

b _ _ _

s _ _ _

c _ _ _

☆ 96 ☆

Name: _____

Draw lines to match.

soil

oil

boil

coil

Which word does not belong?
Fill in the bubble.

1. call ⬭   foil ⬭   coil ⬭

2. boil ⬭   toil ⬭   tail ⬭

3. soil ⬭   all ⬭   oil ⬭

Draw a picture
of your favorite
-oil word.

★ 97
☆

Name: _____

Write words that end with -**own.**

Color each item that ends with -**own.**

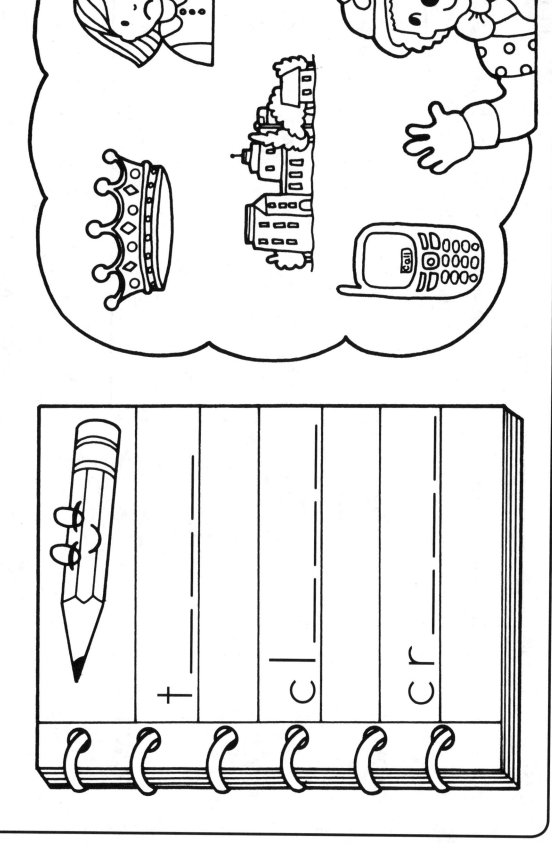

t _ _ _

c l _ _ _

c r _ _ _

Name: _____

Draw lines to match.

clown

town

frown

crown

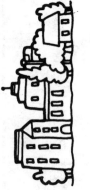

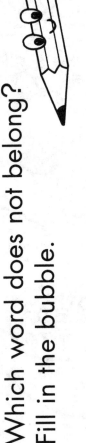

Which word does not belong?
Fill in the bubble.

1. ○ brown   ○ yawn   ○ crown

2. ○ our   ○ town   ○ down

3. ○ frown   ○ clown   ○ claw

Draw a picture
of your favorite
-own word.

Color each item that ends with **-ar**.

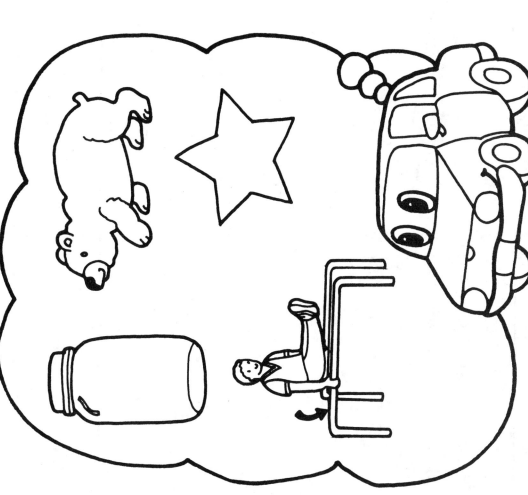

☆ 99
☆☆

Name: _____

Write words that end with **-ar**.

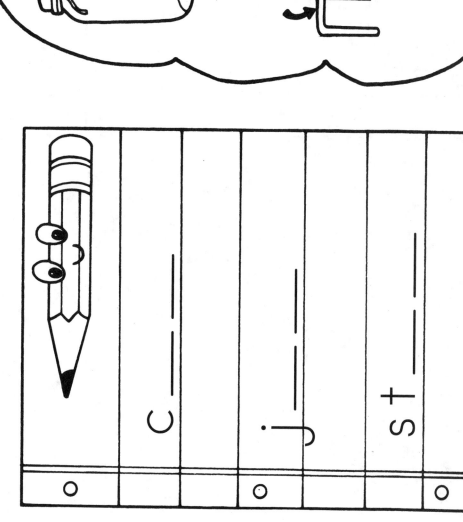

c _ _

j _ _

s t _ _

☆100☆

Name: _____

Draw lines to match.

star

jar

bar

car

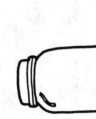

Which word does not belong?
Fill in the bubble.

1. tar ○   tan ○   bar ○

2. far ○   car ○   care ○

3. jar ○   tear ○   scar ○

Draw a picture
of your favorite
-ar word.

☆ 101 ☆

Name: _____

Write words that end with **-ore.**

c _ _ _

s c _ _ _

s n _ _ _

Color each item that ends with **-ore.**

Home Visitors
14   11

☆102☆

Name: _____

Draw lines to match.

core

snore

score

sore

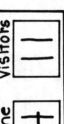

Which word does not belong?
Fill in the bubble.

1. bore ◯   more ◯   bar ◯

2. pore ◯   pole ◯   tore ◯

3. phone ◯   chore ◯   wore ◯

Draw a picture
of your favorite
-ore word.

Name: _____

☆ 103 ☆

Write words that end with **-orn.**

Color each item that ends with **-orn.**

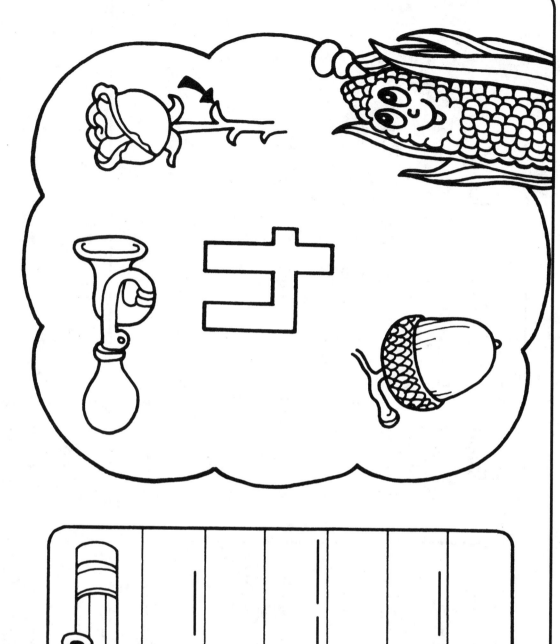

c _ _ _

t h _ _ _

h _ _ _

☆ 104 ☆

Name: _____

Draw lines to match.

horn

corn

thorn

acorn

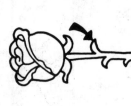
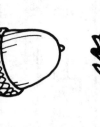

**Which word does not belong?
Fill in the bubble.**

1. torn ◯   barn ◯   born ◯

2. won ◯   worn ◯   thorn ◯

3. morn ◯   corn ◯   more ◯

Draw a picture
of your favorite
-orn word.